CHRISTMAS JOYS

BEST OF
Christmas Joys

BY
JOAN WINMILL BROWN
SELECTED FROM *"CHRISTMAS JOYS"*

A DOUBLEDAY-GALILEE BOOK
DOUBLEDAY & COMPANY, INC.
GARDEN CITY, NEW YORK
1983

Grateful acknowledgment
is made to the following for permission to reprint
their copyrighted material.

Adaptation of "O Holy Night" by Adolphe Adam.
Reprinted by permission of
Novello & Company, Ltd.

"The Quiet People" by Jack D. Martin.
Reprinted by permission from Guideposts magazine.
Copyright © 1966 by Guideposts Associates, Inc.,
Carmel, N.Y. 10512. All rights reserved.

Excerpt from What Is a Family?
by Edith Schaeffer.
Copyright © 1975 by Edith Schaeffer.
Reprinted by permission of the author
and Fleming H. Revell Company.

Excerpt from The Father Christmas Letters
by J. R. R. Tolkien.
Copyright © 1976 by George Allen &
Unwin Publishers, Ltd.
Reprinted by permission of George Allen &
Unwin Publishers, Ltd.
and Houghton Mifflin Company.

LIBRARY OF CONGRESS
CATALOGING IN PUBLICATION DATA
MAIN ENTRY UNDER TITLE:
Best of Christmas joys.
"A Doubleday-Galilee book."
1. Christmas—Miscellanea.   I. Brown, Joan Winmill.
II. Christmas joys.
BV45.B46   1983   242'.33   83-45165
ISBN 0-385-19039-5

ISBN: 0-385-19039-5

Art Direction by Diana Klemin
Book Design by David November
Music Typography by Irwin Rabinowitz

CONTENTS

THE JOY OF TRADITIONS 27

THE JOY OF HOME   39

Christmas!

*T*HE VERY WORD brings joy to our hearts. No matter how we may dread the rush, the long Christmas lists for gifts and cards to be bought and given—when Christmas Day comes there is still the same warm feeling we had as children, the same warmth that enfolds our hearts and our homes.

All over the world people keep the traditions they learned as children. These links with the past cheer us and bring hope for the years that lie ahead. The unbroken chain that binds us to that first Christmas strengthens our faith.

My search for the best in Christmas literature for this anthology led me to many diverse and interesting sources. The vast and majestic Library of Congress in Washington, D.C., the small friendly local libraries, old bookshops, garage sales, books borrowed from friends, all have kept me finding serendipitous contributions.

As I read, I was led into so many different worlds. From the great halls of England in Henry VIII's time to the present, Christmas surrounded me. Charles Dickens' account of a Victorian Christmas escorted me back through the corridors of the past, so that in my imagination I could experience being a guest at the Cratchits' with Tiny Tim and share their meager, but nevertheless joyous, Christmas dinner.

As you share the joys of the many contributors to this book, may your Christmas be filled with happiness.   J.W.B.

THE JOY OF

Silent Night

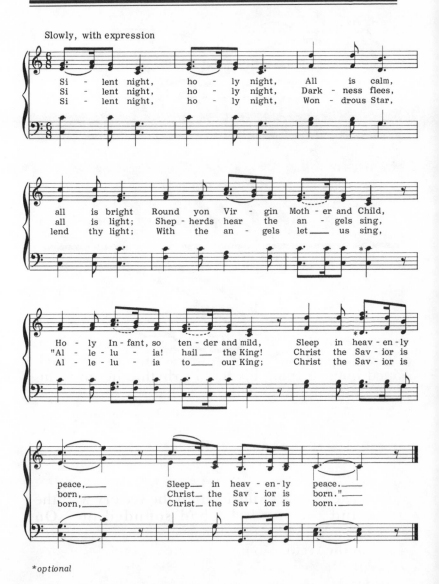

Slowly, with expression

Si - lent night, ho - ly night, All is calm,
Si - lent night, ho - ly night, Dark - ness flees,
Si - lent night, ho - ly night, Won - drous Star,

all is bright Round yon Vir - gin Moth - er and Child,
all is light; Shep - herds hear the an - gels sing,
lend thy light; With the an - gels let us sing,

Ho - ly In - fant, so ten - der and mild, Sleep in heav - en - ly
"Al - le - lu - ia! hail the King! Christ the Sav - ior is
Al - le - lu - ia to our King; Christ the Sav - ior is

peace, Sleep in heav - en - ly peace.
born, Christ the Sav - ior is born."
born, Christ the Sav - ior is born.

*optional

12

JOSEPH MOHR
AND FRANZ GRUBER

*T*HE SONG "SILENT NIGHT" echoed out of the small village of Oberndorf in the Tyrolean Alps of Austria. The twenty-five-year-old rector of the village church, Joseph Mohr, was alone on Christmas Eve, 1818, when he heard a loud pounding on the door. He opened the door and a woman pushed past him gasping, "Come, a child is born, and the young father and mother want you to bless their home." Then the woman collapsed.

The rector started out on a tedious journey up the mountainside, to a small cabin, miles in distance. After many hours of climbing he reached his destination and saw within the cabin a repetition of the Nativity scene. The young woman lay on a bed of boughs, and her newborn son lay in a roughhewn cradle made by the Alpine-mountaineer father. The rector blessed the home and left the cabin to make a return journey to the village. His heart filled with song, because of the uplifting impressive scene; and his ears filled with the rapturous tune which enveloped him. Keeping his feet in rhythm he made his way down the mountainside. That Christmas night the rector stayed up writing the manuscript.

The next morning Joseph Mohr visited the village organist and choirmaster, Franz Gruber. He asked the choirmaster to pick out the melody for the song on an old guitar because the organ was broken. A few hours later Franz Gruber ran to the rectory with the tune and the words he had sounded out. On December 25, 1818, the villagers of Oberndorf gathered in the rectory to hear for the first time the song "Silent Night," sung by Joseph Mohr and Franz Gruber. It was a song of peace.

O LITTLE TOWN OF
Bethlehem

O lit - tle town of Beth - le - hem, How still we see thee lie;
For Christ is born of Ma - ry; And gath - ered all a - bove,
How si - lent - ly, how si - lent - ly, The won - drous gift is giv'n!

A - bove thy deep and dream - less sleep The si - lent stars go by:
While mor - tals sleep, the an - gels keep Their watch of won - d'ring love.
So God im - parts to hu - man hearts The bless - ings of His heav'n.

Yet in thy dark streets shin - eth The ev - er - last - ing Light; The
O morn - ing stars, to - geth - er Pro - claim the ho - ly birth; And
No ear may hear His com - ing, But in this world of sin, Where

hopes and fears of all the years Are met in thee to - night.
prais - es sing to God the King, And peace to men on earth.
meek souls will re - ceive Him, still The dear Christ en - ters in.

*optional

14

PHILLIPS BROOKS

ON CHRISTMAS EVE in Bethlehem in 1865, a young minister was deeply moved by a simple church service commemorating Christ's birth. As he stood in the ancient building, which dated back to the fourth century, little did Phillips Brooks realize that just a few years later the memory of that scene would be used by him to write one of the most beautiful Christmas carols.

In 1868, while minister of Holy Trinity, Philadelphia, he was approached by one of the children who attended the church school to write them a special Christmas song. Sitting down, he remembered the peaceful scene of Bethlehem, with the shepherds' field close by, and in one evening wrote the simple but meaningful verses that tell of God's incredible gift to mankind. Brooks asked his church organist to compose the music—together they gave us a carol that is a favorite in many countries.

O Holy Night

Andante maestoso

O ho-ly night!___ The stars are bright-ly shin - ing, It is the night of the dear Sa-vior's birth; Long lay the world___ in sin and er - ror pin - ing, Till He ap-peared, and the soul felt its worth.

A

ADOLPHE ADAM

A STORY IS TOLD of the effect this beautiful, haunting French carol had during the Franco-Prussian War. French and German soldiers were facing each other in opposite trenches on Christmas Eve, 1870.

Suddenly, a young Frenchman leaped out of his trench and began singing Adolphe Adam's magnificent "Cantique de Noël" (O Holy Night). The Germans were awestruck and not a shot was fired. Then a German climbed out of his trench and sang Martin Luther's Christmas hymn, "From Heaven to Earth I Come."

Adolphe Adam was born in Paris in 1803. Years later, people flocked to the city at Christmastime to hear his popular composition performed in the prominent churches. Originally it was meant for the single voice and even today is one of the most well loved of all Christmas solos.

The original words were written by M. Cappeau de Roquemaure and translated by John S. Dwight.

SECOND VERSE
Led by the light of Faith serenely beaming,
With glowing hearts by His cradle we stand.
So, led by light of a star sweetly gleaming,
Here came the wise men from the Orient land.
The King of Kings lay thus in lowly manger,
In all our trials born to be our friend;
He knows our need, to our weakness no stranger;
Behold your King!
Before the Lowly bend!
Behold your King! your King! before Him bend.

REFRAIN

thrill of hope, the wea - ry world re-joic - es, For yon - der breaks a new and glo - rious morn! Fall on your knees! Oh, hear the an - gel voic - es! O night di - vine, O

18

night,_____ when Christ was born! O night_____ di-vine! O night, O night di-vine! vine! vine!

O COME,
All Ye Faithful
(ADESTE FIDELES)

O come, all ye faith - ful, joy - ful and tri - um - phant, O
Sing, choirs of an - gels, sing in ex - ul - ta - tion, O
Yea, Lord, we greet Thee, born this hap - py morn - ing,

come ye, O come ye to Beth - le - hem;
sing, all ye bright hosts of heav'n a - bove;
Je - sus, to Thee be all glo - ry giv'n;

Come and be - hold Him, born the King of an - gels.
Glo - ry to God, all glo - ry in the high - est.
Word of the Fa - ther, now in flesh ap - pear - ing.

REFRAIN

O come, let us a - dore Him, O come, let us a - dore Him, O

come, let us a - dore Him, Christ, the Lord.

*optional

JOHN FRANCIS WADE

*A*N ENGLISHMAN named John Francis Wade was responsible for bringing this worshipful hymn to us. He traveled throughout Europe copying music for Catholic institutions and families. In Douai, France, he wrote the words and music and included them in a manuscript he was working on at the time. In 1750 it had its first public performance when it was included in the services at the Roman Catholic University in Lisbon.

Thirty-five years later it was sent to the Portuguese Embassy in London and received the name "Portuguese Hymn," after being sung in their chapel. By the Catholics it was called "Adeste, Fideles" and by the Protestants, "O Come, All Ye Faithful," after being translated by Canon Frederick Oakley in 1852.

GOD REST YE MERRY,
Gentlemen

With spirit

God rest ye, mer-ry gen-tle-men, Let noth-ing you dis-may, Re-
From God that is our Fa - ther, The bless-ed An-gels came, Un-

mem-ber Christ our Sa - vior Was born on Christ-mas day, To
to some cer-tain Shep - herds, With tid-ings of the same; That

save poor souls from Sa-tan's pow'r Which had long time gone a-stray.
there was born in Beth - le - hem, The Son of God by name.

REFRAIN

O___ ti - dings of com - fort and joy, com-fort and

joy; O___ ti - dings of com - fort and joy.

*optional

*T*HIS CAROL, full of Christian joy, is one of the most popular in England. It brings to our minds scenes of "Merrie Old England" and probably dates from the sixteenth century. The author is unknown. It was first published in 1846 and harmonized by Sir John Stainer in 1867.

Charles Dickens referred to it in his classic *A Christmas Carol* when a young caroler began to sing, "God bless ye merry, gentleman," through Scrooge's keyhole. "Scrooge seized the ruler with such energy of action that the singer fled in terror, leaving the keyhole to the fog and even more congenial frost."

The word "rest" in the opening line is the Old English term meaning "keep."

We Three Kings
OF ORIENT ARE

Like a processional

We three kings of O - ri - ent are; Bear - ing gifts we
Born a King on Beth - le-hem's plain, Gold I bring to
Frank - in - cense to of - fer have I, In - cense owns a

trav - erse a - far Field and foun - tain, moor and moun - tain,
crown Him a - gain; King for - ev - er, ceas - ing nev - er
De - i - ty nigh; Prayer and prais - ing, all men rais - ing,

REFRAIN

Fol - low - ing yon - der star.
O - ver us all to reign. O,___ star of won - der,
Wor - ship Him, God on high.

star of night, Star with roy - al beau - ty bright, West - ward

lead - ing, still pro - ceed - ing, Guide us to thy per - fect light.

JOHN HENRY HOPKINS, JR.

*T*HIS CAROL conjures up scenes of Christmas pageants, children with home-made crowns and robes, bearing gifts. It has always intrigued young people with the drama of the story. Actually it is a small masterpiece with words and music written by John Henry Hopkins, Jr., in 1857, who was rector of Christ's Church, Williamsport, Pennsylvania.

It is one of the few carols based on the story of the Wise Men in Matthew 2:1–12. The tradition of there being only three Wise Men perhaps was derived from there being three gifts given to the Baby Jesus. The gifts are symbolic of Jesus Christ. Gold stands for Christ's royalty, frankincense for His divinity and myrrh for His suffering.

Through the years there has been established a legend that the Wise Men arrived twelve days after Jesus' birth. Through this developed the custom of Twelfth Night, when gifts are exchanged and the Christmas season comes to a close.

FOURTH VERSE

Myrrh is mine; its bitter perfume
Breathes a life of fathering gloom;
Sorrowing, sighing, bleeding, dying;
Sealed in the stone-cold tomb.
                REFRAIN

FIFTH VERSE

Glorious now behold Him arise,
King, and God, and Sacrifice;
Heav'n sings Alleluia;
Alleluia the earth replies.
                REFRAIN

MAKING YOUR CHRISTMAS
Merry

BILLY GRAHAM

WHEN AT THIS SEASON of the year we wish our friends a "Merry Christmas," it is essential to realize that true merriment of heart is contingent upon the recognition of the truth that Christ was born in Bethlehem for our salvation. The word "merry" is from an old Anglo-Saxon word which sometimes meant "famous," "illustrious," "great," or "mighty." Originally, to be merry did not imply to be merely mirthful, but strong and gallant. It was in this sense that gallant soldiers were called "merry men." Favorable weather was called "merry weather." Brisk winds were called a "merry gale." Spenser speaks of London as "merry London." The word "merry" carries with it the double thought of "might" and "mirth," and is used both ways in Scripture. One of the early Christmas carols was "God Rest You Merry, Gentlemen." The Christian is to engage in spiritual merriment as he thinks upon the fact that, through the redemption, he becomes a child of God's family ... The Bible teaches that the angels made merry at Christ's birth.

THE JOY OF

"Merry Christmas"

JOAN WINMILL BROWN

ARGENTINA	Felices Pascuas
ARMENIA	Schenorhavor Dzenount
BELGIUM (FLEMISH)	Vrolijke Kerstmis
BRAZIL (PORTUGUESE)	Boas Festas
BULGARIA	Chestita Koleda
CHINA	Kung Hsi Hsin Nien or Bing Chu Shen Tan
CZECHOSLOVAKIA	Vesele Vanoce
DENMARK	Glaedelig Jul
ESTONIA	Roomsaid Joulu Puhi
FINLAND	Hauskaa Joulua
FRANCE	Joyeux Noël
GERMANY	Fröhliche Weihnachten
GREECE	Kala Christougena
HOLLAND	Zalig Kerstfeest
HUNGARY	Boldog Karacsony
IRAQ	Idah Saidan Wa Sanah Jadidah
IRELAND (GAELIC)	Nodlaig Nait Cugat
ITALY	Buon Natale

IN MANY
LANGUAGES

JAPAN	Meri Kurisumasu
MEXICO	Feliz Navidad
NORWAY	Gledelig Jul
POLAND	Wesolych Swiat
PORTUGAL	Boas Festas
ROMANIA	Sarbatori Vesele
RUSSIA	S Roshestvóm Khristóvym
SOUTH AFRICA	
(AFRIKAANS)	Een Plesierige Kerfees
SPAIN	Felices Pascuas
SWEDEN	Glad Jul
TURKEY	Noeliniz Ve Yeni Yiliniz Kutlu Olsun
UKRAINE	Chrystos Rozdzajetsia Slawyte Jeho·
WALES	Nadolig Llawen
YUGOSLAVIA	
(CROATIAN)	Srećan Božić
YUGOSLAVIA	
(SERBIAN)	Hristos se rodi

THE IMPORTANCE OF
Traditions

EDITH SCHAEFFER

*O*UR TRADITIONS connected with Christmas are very special. Our four children and their families have their own careful Christmas traditions—some are the same ones we had and some are different ones. For all of our twenty-eight years in Switzerland we have had the five o'clock Christmas Eve service in Champéry, with over a hundred candles to be put in wooden candleholders made of rough logs, and also fastened on fresh green trees. The supper at home has always started with cream of tomato soup with salted whipped cream on top, and has had a main course of easy-to-serve ham and potato chips and salad with special trimmings and homemade rolls. The apple-mince pies with crisscross crusts (or pumpkin if you would rather) are also a traditional dessert. The Christmas tree has been trimmed the night before, during a traditional time of drinking iced ginger ale and eating homemade Christmas cookies spread out in lovely rows on a tray. The Christmas stockings, filled with all sorts of interesting but inexpensive things, are the old hand-knitted stockings our girls wore the first years in Switzerland. Full of holes, but still usable, they add much in the way of memories as they are pulled out one night and filled and then found on Christmas morning. There are always tangerines to be eaten as we come to them, and homemade Christmas bread, along with tea or hot vanilla eggnog to be enjoyed in the bedroom as we open the stockings. The traditional lunch of homemade rolls (filled with thin beef), tomato juice, olives and pickles, and either milk shakes or ginger-ale floats for dessert is eaten whenever we feel hungry, sitting around the Christmas tree, opening gifts. There is the customary reading of Luke 2 and prayer together before eating. For dinner in the evening, there is a traditional tablecloth of lovely thin linen with appliquéd deer on it (bought at a sale in Philadelphia twenty years ago and used every Christmas since).

*T*HERE is something about saying, "We *always* do this," which helps to keep the years together. Time is such an elusive thing that if we keep on meaning to do something interesting, but never do it, year would follow year with no special thoughtfulness being expressed in making gifts, surprises, charming table settings, and familiar, favorite food.

The Royal
CHRISTMAS TREE

THE ILLUSTRATED
LONDON NEWS, 1848

*T*HE CHRISTMAS TREE is annually prepared by Her Majesty's command for the royal children...The tree employed for this festive purpose is a young fir of about eight feet high, and has six tiers of branches. On each tier, or branch, are arranged a dozen wax tapers. Pendant from the branches are elegant trays, baskets, bonbonnières, and other receptacles for sweetmeats of the most varied and expensive kind; and of all forms, colors, and degrees of beauty. Fancy cakes, gilt gingerbread and eggs filled with sweetmeats are also suspended by variously colored ribbons from the branches. The tree, which stands upon a table covered with white damask, is supported at the root by piles of sweets of a larger kind, and by toys and dolls of all descriptions, suited to the youthful fancy...On the summit of the tree stands the small figure of an angel, with outstretched wings, holding in each hand a wreath.

A CHRISTMAS
Tree
FROM "CHRISTMAS STORIES"

CHARLES DICKENS

I HAVE BEEN looking on, this evening, at a merry company of children assembled round that pretty German toy, a Christmas tree. The tree was planted in the middle of a great round table, and towered high above their heads. It was brilliantly lighted by a multitude of little tapers; and everywhere sparkled and glittered with bright objects. There were rosy-cheeked dolls, hiding behind the green leaves; there were real watches (with movable hands, at least, and an endless capacity of being wound up) dangling from innumerable twigs; there were French-polished tables, chairs, bedsteads, wardrobes, eight-day clocks, and various other articles of domestic furniture (wonderfully made, in tin, at Wolverhampton), perched among the boughs, as if in preparation for some fairy housekeeping; there were jolly, broad-faced little men, much more agreeable in appearance than many real men—and no wonder, for their heads took off, and showed them to be full of sugarplums; there were fiddles and drums; there were tambourines, books, workboxes, paint boxes, sweetmeat boxes, peep-show boxes, and all kinds of boxes; there were trinkets for the elder girls, far brighter than any grown-up gold and jewels...there were guns, swords and banners...pen wipers, smelling bottles...real fruit...imitation apples, pears and walnuts, crammed with surprises; in short, as a pretty child, before me, delightedly whispered to another pretty child, "There was everything, and more."

Being now at home again, and alone, the only person in the house awake, my thoughts are drawn back, by a fascination which I do not care to resist, to my own childhood. I begin to consider, what do we all remember best upon the branches of the Christmas tree of our own young Christmas days, by which we climbed to real life?

*S*TRAIGHT, in the middle of the room, cramped in the freedom of its growth by no encircling walls or soon-reached ceiling, a shadowy tree arises; and, looking up into the dreamy brightness of its top—for I observe in this tree the singular property that it appears to grow downward toward the earth—I look into my youngest Christmas recollection...

I see a wonderful row of little lights rise smoothly out of the ground, before a vast green curtain. Now a bell rings—a magic bell, which still sounds in my ears unlike all other bells—and music plays, amid a buzz of voices, and a fragrant smell of orange peel. Anon, the magic bell commands the music to cease, and the great green curtain rolls itself up majestically, and The Play begins...Out of this delight springs the toy theater—there it is, with its familiar proscenium, and ladies in feathers, in the boxes!—and all its attendant occupation with paste and glue, and gum, and water colors, in the getting up of *The Miller and His Men*...

Vast is the crop of such fruit, shining on our Christmas tree; in blossom, almost at the very top; ripening all down the boughs!

Among the later toys and fancies hanging there—

as idle often and less pure—be the images once asso-
ciated with the sweet old Waits, the softened music in
the night, ever unalterable! Encircled by the social
thoughts of Christmastime, still let the benignant figure of my childhood stand unchanged! In every
cheerful image and suggestion that the season brings,
may the bright star that rested above the poor roof be
the star of all the Christian world! A moment's pause,
O vanishing tree, of which the lower branches are
dark to me as yet, and let me look once more! I know
there are blank spaces on thy branches, where eyes
that I have loved have looked and smiled; from which
they are departed. But far above, I see the raiser of
the dead girl, and the widow's son; and God is good!
If age be hiding for me in the unseen portion of thy
downward growth, O may I, with a gray head, turn a
child's heart to that figure yet, and a child's trustful-
ness and confidence!

*N*OW, the tree is decorated with bright merriment, and song, and dance, and cheerfulness.
And they are welcome. Innocent and welcome be they ever held, beneath the branches of the
Christmas tree, which cast no gloomy shadow!

THE CHRISTMAS
Pine Tree

BORIS PASTERNAK

I love her to tears, at sight, from the first,
As she comes from the woods—
*   in storm and snow.*
So awkward her branches, the shyest of firs!
We fashion her threads unhurriedly, slow.
Her garments of silvery gossamer lace,
Patterns of tinsel, and spangles aglow
From branch unto branch down to the base.

FROM "A DAY OF
Pleasant Bread"

DAVID GRAYSON

*T*HEY HAVE ALL GONE NOW, and the house is very still. For the first time this evening I can hear the familiar sound of the December wind blustering about the house, complaining at closed doorways, asking questions at the shutters; but here in my room, under the green reading lamp, it is warm and still. Although Harriet has closed the doors, covered the coals in the fireplace, and said good-night, the atmosphere still seems to tingle with the electricity of genial humanity.

The parting voice of the Scotch preacher still booms in my ears:

"This," said he, as he was going out of our door, wrapped like an Arctic highlander in cloaks and tippets, "has been a day of pleasant bread."

One of the very pleasantest I can remember!

I sometimes think we expect too much of Christmas Day. We try to crowd into it the long arrears of kindliness and humanity of the whole year. As for me, I like to take my Christmas a little at a time, all through the year. And thus I drift along into the holidays—let them overtake me unexpectedly—waking up some fine morning and suddenly saying to myself:

"Why, this is Christmas Day!"

THE JOY OF

Home

God Bless
THE MASTER OF
THIS HOUSE

AUTHOR UNKNOWN

God bless the master of this house,
The mistress also,
And all the little children
That round the table go:

And all your kin and kinsfolk
That dwell both far and near;
We wish you a merry Christmas,
And a happy New Year.

Christmas Speech, 1941

WINSTON CHURCHILL

While Winston Churchill was staying at the White House, Christmas 1941—during World War II—he delivered this speech to the American people:

SPEND THIS ANNIVERSARY and festival far from my country, far from my family, and yet I cannot truthfully say that I feel far from home. Whether it be the ties of blood on my mother's side, or the friendships I have developed here over many years of active life, or the commanding sentiment of comradeship in the common cause of great peoples who speak the same language, who kneel at the same altars and, to a very large extent, pursue the same ideals; I cannot feel myself a stranger here in the center and at the summit of the United States. I feel a sense of unity and fraternal association which, added to the kindliness of your welcome, convinces me that I have a right to sit at your fireside and share your Christmas joys.

Fellow workers, fellow soldiers in the cause, this is a strange Christmas Eve. Almost the whole world is locked in deadly struggle. Armed with the most terrible weapons which science can devise, the nations advance upon each other. Ill would it be for us this Christmastide if we were not sure that no greed for the lands or wealth of any other people, no vulgar ambitions, no morbid lust for material gain at the expense of others had led us to the field. Ill would it be for us if that were so. Here, in the midst of war, raging and roaring over all the lands and seas, sweeping nearer to our hearths and homes; here, amid all these tumults, we have tonight the peace of the spirit in each cottage home and in every generous heart. Therefore we may cast aside, for this night at least, the cares and dangers which beset us and make for the children an evening of happiness in a world of storm. Here then, for one night only, each home throughout the English-speaking world should be a brightly lighted island of happiness and peace.

*L*ET the children have their night of fun and laughter, let the gifts of Father Christmas delight their play. Let us grown-ups share to the full in their unstinted pleasures before we turn again to the stern tasks and the formidable years that lie before us, resolved that by our sacrifice and daring these same children shall not be robbed of their inheritance or denied their right to live in a free and decent world.

And so, in God's mercy, a happy Christmas to you all.

FROM A LETTER WRITTEN BY GENERAL ROBERT E. LEE

To His Wife

DECEMBER 25, 1861

I CANNOT LET THIS DAY of grateful rejoicing pass without some communion with you. I am thankful for the many among the past that I have passed with you, and the remembrance of them fills me with pleasure. As to our old home, if not destroyed it will be difficult ever to be recognized.

…It is better to make up our minds to a general loss. They cannot take away the remembrances of the spot, and the memories of those that to us rendered it sacred. That will remain to us as long as life will last and that we can preserve…

Christmas Eve

KATE DOUGLAS WIGGIN

The door is on the latch tonight,
The hearth-fire is aglow,
I seem to hear soft passing feet—
The Christ child in the snow.

My heart is open wide tonight
For stranger, kith or kin.
I would not bar a single door
Where Love might enter in.

THE JOY OF

Children

FROM "A CHRISTMAS CAROL"

Tiny Tim

CHARLES DICKENS
RETOLD BY HIS GRANDDAUGHTER
MARY ANGELA DICKENS

IT WILL SURPRISE YOU all very much to hear that there was once a man who did not like Christmas. In fact, he had been heard on several occasions to use the word *humbug* with regard to it. His name was Scrooge, and he was a hard, sour-tempered man of business, intent only on saving and making money, and caring nothing for anyone. He paid the poor, hardworking clerk in his office as little as he could possibly get the work done for, and lived on as little as possible himself, alone, in two dismal rooms. He was never merry or comfortable, or happy, and he hated other people to be so, and that was the reason why he hated Christmas, because people *will* be happy at Christmas, you know, if they possibly can, and like to have a little money to make themselves and others comfortable.

Well, it was Christmas Eve, a very cold and foggy one, and Mr. Scrooge, having given his poor clerk unwilling permission to spend Christmas Day at home, locked up his office and went home himself in a very bad temper, and with a cold in his head. After having taken some gruel as he sat over a miserable fire in his dismal room, he got into bed, and had some wonderful and disagreeable dreams, to which we will leave him, while we see how Tiny Tim, the son of his poor clerk, spent Christmas Day.

The name of this clerk was Bob Cratchit. He had a wife

and five other children besides Tim, who was a weak and delicate little cripple, and for this reason was dearly loved by his father, and the rest of the family; not but what he was a dear little boy too, gentle and patient and loving, with a sweet face of his own, which no one could help looking at.

*W*HENEVER he could spare the time, it was Mr. Cratchit's delight to carry his little boy out on his shoulder to see the shops and the people; and today he had taken him to church for the first time.

"Whatever has got your precious father, and your brother Tiny Tim!" exclaimed Mrs. Cratchit. "Here's dinner all ready to be dished up. I've never known him so late on Christmas Day before."

"Here he is, Mother!" cried Belinda, and "Here he is!" cried the other children as Mr. Cratchit came in, his long comforter hanging three feet from under his threadbare coat; for cold as it was, the poor clerk had no topcoat. Tiny Tim was perched on his father's shoulder with his little crutch in his hand.

"And how did Tim behave?" asked Mrs. Cratchit.

"As good as gold and better," replied the father. "I think, wife, the child gets thoughtful, sitting at home so much. He told me, coming home, that he hoped the people in church who saw he was a cripple would be pleased to remember on Christmas Day Who it was who made the lame to walk."

"Bless his sweet heart!" said his mother in a trembling voice, and the father's voice trembled too, as he remarked that Tiny Tim was growing strong and hearty at last.

Dinner was waiting to be dished up. Mrs. Cratchit proudly placed a goose upon the table. Belinda brought in the apple sauce, and Peter the mashed potatoes; the other children set chairs, Tim's as usual, close to his father's; and Tim was so excited that he rapped the table with his knife, and cried "Hurrah!" After the goose came the pudding, with a great smell of steam, like washing day, as it came out of the copper; in it came, all ablaze, with its sprig of holly

47

in the middle, and was eaten to the last morsel. Then apples and oranges were set upon the table, and a shovelful of chestnuts on the fire, and Mr. Cratchit served round some hot sweet stuff out of a jug as they closed round the fire, and said, "A Merry Christmas to us all, my dears. God bless us!" "God bless us every one!" echoed Tiny Tim, and then they drank each other's health, and Mr. Scrooge's health, and told stories and sang songs—Tim, who had a sweet little voice, singing, very well indeed, a song about a child who was lost in the snow on Christmas Day.

*N*OW I TOLD YOU that Mr. Scrooge had some disagreeable and wonderful dreams on Christmas Eve, and so he had; and in one of them he dreamt that a Chistmas spirit showed him his clerk's home; he saw them all gathered round the fire, and heard them drink his health, and Tiny Tim's song, and he took special note of Tiny Tim himself.

In his dreams that night Scrooge visited all sorts of places and saw all sorts of people, for different spirits came to him and led him about where they would, and presently he was taken again to his poor clerk's home. The mother was doing some needlework, seated by the table; a tear dropped on it now and then, and she said, poor thing, that the work, which was black, hurt her eyes. The children sat, sad and silent, about the room, except Tiny Tim, who was not there. Upstairs the father, with his face hidden in his hands, sat beside a little bed, on which lay a tiny figure, white and still. "My little child, my pretty little child," he sobbed, as the tears fell through his fingers onto the floor. "Tiny Tim died because his father was too poor to give him what was necessary to make him well; *you* kept him poor," said the dream spirit to Mr. Scrooge. The father kissed the cold, little face on the bed, and went downstairs, where the sprays of holly still remained about the humble room; and, taking his hat, went out, with a wistful glance at the little crutch in the corner as he shut the door. Mr. Scrooge saw all this, and many more things as strange and sad—the spirit took care of that; but, wonderful to relate, he woke next morning feeling a different man—feeling as he had never felt in his life before.

"Why, I am as light as a feather, and as happy as an angel, and as merry as a schoolboy," he said to himself. "A Merry Christmas to everybody! A happy New Year to all the world." And a few minutes later he was ordering a turkey to be taken round to Tiny Tim's house, a turkey so large that the man who took it had to go in a cab.

Next morning poor Bob Cratchit crept into the office a few minutes late, expecting to be roundly abused and scolded for it; he soon found, however, that his master was a very different man to the one who had grudged him his Christmas holiday, for there was Scrooge telling him heartily he was going to raise his salary and asking quite affectionately after Tiny Tim! "And mind you make up a good fire in your room before you set to work, Bob," he said, as he closed his own door.

BOB COULD HARDLY BELIEVE his eyes and ears, but it was all true, and more prosperous times came to his family, and happier, for Tiny Tim did not die—not a bit of it. Mr. Scrooge was a second father to him from that day; he wanted for nothing, and grew up strong and hearty. Mr. Scrooge loved him, and well he might, for was it not Tiny Tim who had unconsciously, through the Christmas dream spirit, touched his hard heart, and caused him to be a good and happy man.

Yes, Virginia,
THERE IS A SANTA CLAUS

THE NEW YORK "SUN"

*L*ITTLE VIRGINIA O'HANLON was very upset when she was told by her friends that there was no such thing as Santa Claus. When she asked her father, he did not want to give her a straight answer. Remembering that he always wrote to the New York *Sun* for advice about any question that came up in the family regarding how to pronounce a word, or a historical fact, Virginia decided to write a letter to the editor.

Her letter and the consequent reply have been cherished down through the years:

The New York *Sun,* September 21, 1897

We take pleasure in answering at once and thus prominently the communication below, expressing at the same time our great gratification that its faithful author is numbered among the friends of *The Sun:*

Dear Editor:

I am 8 years old.

Some of my little friends say there is no Santa Claus.

Papa says "If you see it in *The Sun* it's so."

Please tell me the truth, is there a Santa Claus?

Virginia O'Hanlon
115 West 95th Street

*V*IRGINIA, your little friends are wrong. They have been affected by the skepticism of a skeptical age. They do not believe except what they see. They think that nothing can be which is not comprehensible by their little minds. All minds, Virginia, whether they be men's or children's, are little. In this great universe of ours man is a mere insect, an ant, in his intellect, as compared with the boundless world about him, as measured by the intelligence capable of grasping the whole of truth and knowledge.

Yes, Virginia, there is a Santa Claus. He exists as certainly as love and generosity and devotion exist, and you know that they abound and give to your life its highest beauty and joy. Alas! how dreary would be the world if there were no Santa Claus! It would be as dreary as if there were no Virginias. There would be no childlike faith then, no poetry, no romance to make tolerable this existence. We should have no enjoyment, except in sense and sight. The eternal light with which childhood fills the world would be extinguished.

*N*OT BELIEVE IN SANTA CLAUS! You might as well not believe in fairies! You might get your papa to hire men to watch in all the chimneys on Christmas Eve to catch Santa Claus, but even if they did not see Santa Claus coming down, what would that prove? Nobody sees Santa Claus, but that is no sign that there is no Santa Claus. The most real things in the world are those that neither children nor men can see. Did you ever see fairies dancing on the lawn? Of course not, but that's no proof that they are not there. Nobody can conceive or imagine all the wonders there are unseen and unseeable in the world.

*Y*OU TEAR APART the baby's rattle and see what makes the noise inside, but there is a veil covering the unseen world which not the strongest man, nor even the united strength of all the strongest men that ever lived, could tear apart. Only faith, fancy, poetry, love, romance, can push aside that curtain and view and picture the supernal beauty and glory beyond. Is it all real? Ah, Virginia, in all this world there is nothing else real and abiding.

No Santa Claus! Thank God he lives, and he lives forever. A thousand years from now, Virginia, nay, ten times ten thousand years from now, he will continue to make glad the heart of childhood.

Christmas Day:
POSTSCRIPTS BY ILBERETH

J. R. R. TOLKIEN

*J*R. R. TOLKIEN, author of *The Lord of the Rings, The Hobbit,* etc., and Professor of English Language and Literature at Oxford, England, used to write letters filled with imagination and humor from Father Christmas (Santa Claus) to his children each year. They not only looked forward to receiving their gifts, but also to a communication from the North Pole. The four children would find the letters in the house after Father Christmas' visit, or sometimes the postman brought them.

Each year they learned more of Father Christmas' house, his reindeer, Snow-elves, Red Gnomes, Snow men, Cave-bears, the North Polar Bear and his nephews. The Polar Bear was the chief assistant, but eventually Father Christmas employed an Elf named Ilbereth as his secretary. This Elf helped arm the house against an attack of Goblins, and later wrote the following poem about Polar Bear!

Now Christmas day has come round again—
and poor Polar Bear has got a bad pain!

They say he's swallowed a couple of pounds
of nuts without cracking the shells! It sounds
a Polarish sort of thing to do —
but that isn't all, between me and you:
he's eaten a ton of various goods
and recklessly mixed all his favorite foods,
honey with ham, and turkey and treacle,
and pickles with milk. I think that a week'll
be needed to put the old bear on his feet.
And I mustn't forget his particular treat:
plum pudding with sausages and turkish delight
covered with cream and devoured at a bite!
And after this dish, he stood on his head —
it's rather a wonder the poor fellow's not dead!

And here is Polar Bear's reply:

Absolute rot:
I have not got
A pain in my pot.
I do not eat
Turkey or meat:
I stick to the sweet.
Which is why
(As all know) I
Am so sweet myself
You thinnuous elf!
*   Goodby!*

THE JOY OF

Giving

Somehow
NOT ONLY FOR
CHRISTMAS

JOHN GREENLEAF WHITTIER

Somehow not only for Christmas
But all the long year through,
The joy that you give to others
Is the joy that comes back to you.

And the more you spend in blessing
The poor and lonely and sad,
The more of your heart's possessing
Returns to make you glad.

AN EXCERPT FROM A

Letter

WRITTEN TO JAMES GARFIELD'S GRANDSON
DECEMBER 26, 1902

THEODORE ROOSEVELT

YESTERDAY Archie got among his presents a small rifle from me and a pair of riding boots from his mother. He won't be able to use the rifle until next summer, but he has gone off very happy in the riding boots for a ride on the calico pony Algonquin, the one you rode the other day.

A GLIMPSE OF
Christmas Gifts
FROM
THE PAST...

GEORGE WASHINGTON

OR THE CHRISTMAS OF 1759, President George Washington wrote the following list of presents he wished to give his stepchildren, five-year-old John and three-year-old Patsy.

A bird on Bellows
A Cuckoo
A turnabout Parrot
A Grocers Shop
An Aviary
A Prussian Dragoon
A Man Smoakg
A Tunbridge Tea Sett
3 Neat Tunbridge Toys
A Neat Book fash Tea Chest
A box best Household Stuff
A straw Patch box w. a Glass
A neat dress'd Wax Baby

Letter
TO
HANS CHRISTIAN
ANDERSEN
DECEMBER 1847

CHARLES DICKENS

A THOUSAND THANKS, my dear Andersen, for your kind and dearly prized remembrance of me in your Christmas book. I am very proud of it, and feel deeply honored by it, and I cannot tell you how much I esteem so generous a mark of recollection from a man of such genius as you possess.

Your book made my Christmas fireside happier. We were all charmed with it. The little boy, and the old man, and the pewter soldier are my particular favorites. I read that story over and over again, with the most unspeakable delight.

A Special Gift

HELEN KELLER

THE FIRST CHRISTMAS after Miss Sullivan came to Tuscumbia was a great event...Christmas Eve, after I had hung my stocking. I lay awake a long time, pretending to be asleep and keeping alert to see what Santa Claus would do when he came. At last I fell asleep with a new doll and a white bear in my arms. Next morning it was I who waked the whole family with my first "Merry Christmas!" I found surprises, not in the stocking only, but on the table, on all the chairs, at the door, on the very windowsill; indeed, I could hardly walk without stumbling on a bit of Christmas wrapped up in tissue paper. But when my teacher presented me with a canary, my cup of happiness overflowed.

Little Tim was so tame that he would hop on my finger and eat candied cherries out of my hand. Miss Sullivan taught me to take all the care of my new pet. Every morning after breakfast, I prepared his bath, made his cage clean and sweet, filled his cups with fresh seed and water from the well-house, and hung a spray of chickweed in his swing.

The Real Spirit
OF CHRISTMAS

CALVIN COOLIDGE

CHRISTMAS IS NOT a time nor a season, but a state of mind. To cherish peace and goodwill, to be plenteous in mercy, is to have the real spirit of Christmas.

Special Delivery

MRS. CHARLES STEPHAN

BASED ON A "MEMPHIS COMMERCIAL APPEAL" NEWS STORY BY JACK MARTIN

*D*ELIVERY BOYS come in all shapes and sizes—and in a variety of speeds and attitudes too. Some come to the door like beleaguered deliverers of doom while others come on the bound, as though there were more rewards to work than the pay.

David Ward, of Memphis, Tennessee, is the latter kind. Weekdays after school and Saturdays, David pedals his bike for the Speedway Drug Store. And David's a good sort for the job. When he delivers a prescription and says, "I hope you're feeling better" in that polite, concerned way of his, somehow you *do* feel better.

Last year on a Saturday night before Christmas, David, who was thirteen then, received his weekly salary as usual. But he didn't go home. He had a special delivery of his own to make.

First he went down to the lot were the Christmas trees were being sold. When he'd given a number of the trees his careful inspection, he bought one and loaded it on his bicycle. Then he wheeled it over to

605 Life Street, the home of a steady customer, Mrs. Brady Neals. She was seventy-one. And she had been blind for thirty-seven years.

"It's me, Mrs. Neals, David from Speedway," he said when she came to the door. And then David walked in and set up the tree and talked cheerily as he trimmed it with the lights and decorations he had brought along.

*M*RS. NEALS COULD HARDLY SPEAK. Even as David was leaving she could only mumble her thanks. But the old lady was thrilled. She kept reaching out to touch the tree's branches and to breathe its forest-fresh fragrance. "I'm seventy-one years old," she kept saying over and over, "I'm seventy-one years old and I've never had a tree."

Delivery boys come in all shapes and sizes and some of them bring more to their jobs than work.